"What would you have if you had the playful intricacy of Mozart, the intuitive rigour of Wittgenstein, and John Muir's love of the earth? You would have the poetry of Jan Zwicky."

— ROO BORSON

"Whereof one cannot speak, thereof one must be silent. Or so we have heard. Perhaps, however, there are ways of speaking that do not break the silence, but rather invite the silence itself to come to voice. Jan Zwicky is an exquisite poet-philosopher with a classical musician's feel for the rhythm and melody of genuine thought; we sometimes feel the ground breathing through her as she thinks and dreams."

— DAVID ABRAM

"[A] unique poet-philosopher and intellectual pioneer.... Trained as an analytic philosopher and a brilliant Wittgensteinian, Zwicky has the poet's ability to question her own assertions at every step, showing us that 'everything we see could also be otherwise'."

— MARJORIE PERLOFF

"Jan Zwicky's calling as a philosopher has been to rethink what philosophical thinking consists of."

— DENNIS LEE, "The Music of Thinking," in *Lyric Ecology: An Appreciation of the Work of Jan Zwicky*, edited by Mark Dickinson and Clare Goulet

WITTGENSTEIN ELEGIES

Jan Zwicky

Wittgenstein Elegies

with a new afterword by the author
and a new introduction
by Sue Sinclair

BRICK BOOKS

ISBN 978-1-77131-347-6

We acknowledge the Canada Council for the Arts and the Ontario Arts
Council for their support of our publishing program.

BRICK BOOKS
431 Boler Road, Box 20081
London, Ontario N6K 4G6

www.brickbooks.ca

LIBRARY AND ARCHIVES CANADA CATALOGUING IN PUBLICATION

Zwicky, Jan, 1955–, author
     Wittgenstein elegies / Jan Zwicky ; with a new afterword by the author
and a new introduction by Sue Sinclair. — Revised edition.

(Brick Books classics ; 6)
Poems.
Originally published: Coldstream [Ont.] : Brick Books, © 1986.
ISBN 978-1-77131-347-6 (pbk.)

     1. Wittgenstein, Ludwig, 1889–1951 — Poetry.   I. Sinclair, Sue, 1972–,
writer of introduction   II. Title.   III. Series: Brick Books classics ; 6

PS8599.W53W57 2015   C811'.54   C2015-900187-0

CONTENTS

1 · *On Misunderstanding*

> [I]t is VERY *hard not to be understood by a single soul!*
> — Wittgenstein in a letter to Bertrand Russell, August 19, 1919[1]

Over his lifetime Wittgenstein more than once expressed a fear of being misunderstood. He seems to have found the prospect unbearably painful. The lines above are from a letter to Bertrand Russell, written after Frege, one of the few people Wittgenstein had hoped would grasp the sense of his *Tractatus Logico-Philosophicus,* proved unsympathetic. If meaning really is "like going up to someone" – one of Wittgenstein's most striking insights – we might say that he was afraid that no one would know what to make of his style of approach.[2] In "The Geology of Norway," a companion poem to *Wittgenstein Elegies,* Zwicky imagines him asking about the plains and deserts of the very Earth itself, "And will they understand? / Will they have a name for us?"[3]

Sadly, Wittgenstein's fear was often realized. Perhaps the most significant misunderstanding he endured was the one that made him a hero of the Logical Positivist movement. The *Tractatus* seemed to Positivists to confirm that only the world of so-called facts, expressed in logically coherent propositions, offered any real meaning, whereas, as Zwicky says, "it was actually an attempt to demonstrate that all things of value utterly supersede the world of 'facts'" (note to "Philosopher's Stone"). The point was to show limits on the meaning that logic could compass, not to enshrine logic as the very seat of meaning. Zwicky again: "Analysis was never meant to hold / or judge: a purifier of the ore / it cannot comprehend."

In her afterword to this edition Zwicky tells us that as an undergraduate, she felt that the Wittgenstein she was presented with at school was not the Wittgenstein she found on the page. *Wittgenstein Elegies*, then, is partly an effort to draw out the Wittgenstein she encountered; it offers us a way of understanding his work, joins him in gesturing toward aspects of the world that defy parsing into propositions but are meaningful nonetheless.

In light of this effort, I can't help but feel that the poem – for despite the plural title, it does function as one long poem – is partly for Wittgenstein as well as for the rest of us. It is his ally. Zwicky says in her afterword that she "ventriloquizes" Wittgenstein. This puts her in ethically dangerous territory: adopting someone else's voice is fraught with the possibility of misrepresenting him and usurping his autonomy. But it feels to me that when speaking *as* Wittgenstein Zwicky is more fundamentally speaking *to* him, in our presence. The *Elegies* seem a kind of "reflective listening," to borrow a term from therapeutic practice. The reflective listener makes no claim beyond that of listening seriously – attending to tone, mood, gestures both linguistic and physical – then reflecting these back to the speaker. This listening is helpful in no small measure because it offers the comfort of empathic attention, the dignity of being heard. Seen as an effort of reflective listening, the poem mirrors Wittgenstein's life and thought *as if* back to him. Though it's impossible to offer Wittgenstein such a gift in actuality, the *Elegies* nevertheless seem to me a gesture of consolation across the years – not in fact able to put an arm around him but wanting to.

Why bother with such a gesture if it can't be received? A few reasons occur to me. One is that the dead may be afforded dignity if not comfort. Another is that if offered even to the dead, care may flourish as an impulse and develop as a skill. Another,

not unrelated to care, is that reading *Wittgenstein Elegies* makes
me want to be a better listener.

2 · *Philosophy as Poetry*

> *I think I summed up my attitude to philosophy when I said:*
> *philosophy ought really to be written as a* poetic composition.
> — Wittgenstein[4]

It was through poetry that Wittgenstein demonstrated his di-
vergence from the Vienna Circle, the beating heart of Logical
Positivism: convinced to attend some of their meetings, he more
than once turned his back on the group and read poems aloud.[5]
I picture Wittgenstein as consoled by Zwicky's *Elegies* partly
because he might have been relieved to see his work taken up
in and as poetry.

His biographer Ray Monk observes that Wittgenstein's style
"was curiously at odds with his subject-matter, as though a poet
had strayed into the analysis of the foundations of mathematics
and the Theory of Meaning."[6] But what does it mean to call a
philosopher a poet or poet-like? And what does it mean to write
a philosophical work as a "poetic composition"? In the *Elegies,*
Zwicky begins to respond to such questions, and continues to
explore them in *Lyric Philosophy* and *Wisdom & Metaphor.* The
Elegies not only build on Wittgenstein's images and metaphors
(the tools, the ladder, the family, the room in which even the
dust has its place), but it also honours the aphoristic, resonant
quality of his thought, fragmentary without being disunified.
The *Elegies* set a variety of voices, passages, thoughts and im-
ages side by side to reveal the resonances they bear in each
other's presence; the poem allows meaning to move between
them without proscribing or regulating that movement. *Lyric*

Philosophy, which Zwicky published on the heels of *Wittgenstein Elegies,* argues that sensitivity to resonance is a kind of thought; insofar as poetry is structured by resonances, it is a way of thinking. Inspired by Wittgenstein, the *Elegies* implicitly argue the same thing.

Each time I read Zwicky's "The Death of Georg Trakl," I am moved by the character Wittgenstein's despairing admiration of the poet:

> *I cannot help these words as he can:*
> *mute radiance, the empty shining valley.*
> *I cannot keep them clean, they suffocate,*
> *fall stillborn from my mouth.*
> *Prod them for signs of life like poisoned mice.*

It's not clear that the real Wittgenstein, although Trakl's patron, understood his poetry.[7] But regardless of whether or not the real Wittgenstein 'got' Trakl's poems, we can imagine with Zwicky that he saw how Trakl "helped" words, and we can picture his despair at failing them, his poisoned mice. This would be a particularly bitter realization given Wittgenstein's deep desire to heal, to assuage misunderstanding. Zwicky allows him to see and to admire the paradoxical "mute radiance" of Trakl's words – their revealing silence. For although the last lines of the *Tractatus* tell us that "[w]hereof one cannot speak, thereof one must be silent," Zwicky shows that there is yet a way of speaking that leaves room for what can't be said. She quotes Trakl:

> *When autumn has come*
> *A sober clarity appears in the grove.*
> *Calmed we wander beside red walls*
> *And our round eyes follow the flight of birds.*

3 · *Clarity*

What can be said at all can be said clearly.
— Wittgenstein's preface to the *Tractatus*

The substance of the world is light,
is water: here, clear
even when it's dying
— Zwicky, from "Practising Bach" in *Forge*

It's hardly surprising that Zwicky, poet, philosopher and classical musician, would have the kind of affinity for Wittgenstein (also a lover of classical music) that resulted in the *Elegies*. But the deepest point of contact I feel between them has less to do with any particular activity than it does their shared love of clarity. The Wittgenstein of the *Tractatus* writes that "the object of philosophy is the logical clarification of thoughts,"[8] though the later Wittgenstein may have been more inclined to Zwicky's description of philosophy as "thinking in love with clarity."[9]

In her foreword to the *Elegies* Zwicky quotes from final papers in which Wittgenstein describes his work as written for those who share his "striving after clarity and perspicuity in no matter what structure." He couldn't have hoped for a reader more sympathetic in this sense than Zwicky: however her work has varied over the years, from the philosophically dense *Elegies* to her lighter-than-air small songs, love of clarity has been a constant. But if the clarity of an analytically rigourous work like the *Tractatus* is not easily achieved, neither is that of an elegy. How to coax words toward transparency, how to let language become silence's echo chamber? As Zwicky's Wittgenstein asks, "How does one build / a living face?" Though there's no easy answer, Zwicky's adjustments in this version of the *Elegies* are a lesson for anyone interested in the craft of clarity.

Most obviously, the various voices are now more readily

13

distinguished thanks to names added in the margins, though the separation of these names from the flow of the poem allows the voices to remain integrated. Most of the other changes are a matter of fine-tuning, but they bear on meaning. To wit, compare in the first edition, "So much is constant: / Desk, cot, window, soft grey wood, light, sea," to this in the second edition: "So much is constant: / desk, cot, window. Wood, light, sea." It's not uncommon for writers to pare away adjectives – which Zwicky does several times in this revision – but notice what is achieved in this instance by dropping "soft grey." The pace is more even – more constant – without the quickening introduced by "soft grey." The introduction of the extra period also evokes a new, felt sense of constancy: three constants, full stop, three constants, full stop. The revised lines simply *are* more constant.

Other small revisions simplify the language. "[T]he hands of little children" becomes "small hands"; "winter mornings with sunshine / Unrecoverable" turns into "winter mornings sunlit, / unrecoverable". Zwicky's phrasing is also plainer, more natural: "No longer rest / Your weight upon the earth" changes to "Don't rest / your weight on earth". Here, notice again the effect of sound on meaning: in part because of the line break, I'm inclined to read these as iambs ("don't REST / your WEIGHT on EARTH"), which means that emphasis lands only on "rest," weight" and "earth." There are no longer emphases on less important syllables ("LON-ger" and "ON" in the original). When meaning is a matter of resonance and requires the integration of every aspect of what's said, such slight changes can alter the whole structure – the way a shift in the way you're holding your shoulders can release the tension in your whole body.

"This was our mistake."
— Zwicky in "Confessions," quoting the *Investigations*

My own confession: when I first read *Wittgenstein Elegies,* I found it difficult. There were passages that resonated deeply for me, "The Death of Georg Trakl" in particular. But at the time I had read only a little philosophy, and I think that's why other parts were more opaque to me, particularly "Confessions." This section, less biographical than the others, less imagistic, is composed almost entirely of alternating passages from Wittgenstein's two published works, the *Tractatus Logico-Philosophicus* and the *Philosophical Investigations,* and it may be best appreciated by readers who have the background to make head or tail of statements like *"Essence is shown in general form."* I say "may" because although philosophically dense, it moves in a way that readers of poetry will likely recognize and feel at home in.

In his introduction to the *Investigations* Wittgenstein says that "it suddenly seemed to me I should publish those old thoughts and the new ones together: that the latter could be seen in the right light only by contrast with and against the background of my old way of thinking."[10] In the *Elegies,* and in "Confessions" in particular, Zwicky does what he dreamed: she brings together the old thoughts and the new, juxtaposing fragments of each in a way that Wittgenstein himself does only once in the *Investigations* (he quotes and responds to his *Tractatus* in fragment 1.14, which Zwicky reproduces in "Confessions"). It's partly this resonance-sensitive structure and the way it invites the mind to move that I imagine appealing to readers accustomed to poetry.

The exact nature of the relationship between the earlier and later Wittgensteins is a matter of some dispute. "Confessions" reveals several points of friction between them. For example: to say that "[l]iving speech is not a form of calculus" (*Investigations*) is to approach language very differently from one who says, *"Propositions are truth-functions of assertions of prime facts,"* (*Tractatus*). Zwicky brings these statements together, marking the contrast. But the *Tractatus*-era Wittgenstein who believes in the silent manifestation of meaning is not so far from the *Investigations*-era Wittgenstein who sees language as gestural at heart. A belief in meaning-beyond-propositions and even meaning-beyond-language is common to both Wittgensteins, and this spirit animates the *Elegies* as a whole.

Beyond addressing the question of the differences and continuities between Wittgenstein's two books, "Confessions" also shows that the later Wittgenstein didn't only reveal the flaws in his earlier thinking. He also spoke to the desire that underlies them, spoke with empathy and understanding. Hence the "we" and the revealing use of the present tense in this passage in the voice of the older Wittgenstein:

> *We are seduced.*
> *We think it must be in reality,*
> *we think already that we see it there.*
> *A thing that we had always known*
> *but never spoken.*
> *This was our mistake.*

Zwicky highlights the compassion the later Wittgenstein shows for the desire of his younger self, a desire shared by most of philosophy: "We have yearned for speech / designed for gods, a highway to the truth. / In front of us it shimmers. But of course / we cannot use it. It is permanently closed." His tone is, well, elegiac: if only we *could* speak like the gods.

For my money, the most beautiful, most powerful moment of the "Confessions" is its end, the release into the utterly lyric voice. And it does feel like a release: the rushing river of philosophy reaches the delta, drops its weighty sediment and lets meaning float out past argument into a silent beholding of the world, its "[b]lue, blue" water. This is what I imagine readers of poetry will be alive to, will find meaningful if they allow themselves to push through some of the more puzzling philosophical language. Even while coming up against the difficulty of the quoted passages, I can feel the meaning of the movement through them and into the lyric voice. The build-up of philosophical tension followed by its release makes me feel that the language Wittgenstein was reaching for was poetry, and that what poetry reaches for is silence.

The tension doesn't entirely dissolve in these last lines, but it changes shape. As the more purely lyric voice comes to the fore – a way of thinking grounded in what is seen and felt, in image, rhythm and repetition – there emerges a regretful acceptance of the limits of language, and a difficult kind of peace. Can we say anything adequate to the unuttering landscape, its mountains, mist and shore? No, but we can try to speak in a way that makes us available to its silence. When we think of the *Tractatus* as, in Zwicky's words, "a sequence of variations on silence," it's no wonder he had trouble using language in a way that would both allow for silence and let him be understood by philosophers who didn't share – indeed seemed incapable of sharing – his sense of speechlessness before what matters most.[11]

5 · Why Elegies?

> There is nothing left to strip away, grind
> down, wear off: but still not pure enough, no
> clarity.
> —Zwicky in "Rosro, County Galway"

Perhaps I've already said enough that an answer to this question is obvious, though I've said nothing of Wittgenstein's overbearing father, of his brothers' suicides, of his own suicidal impulses, of his experiences on the front in the First World War....

But beyond such circumstances – and no doubt on account of some of them – is his fear of being misunderstood. And the extent to which he *was* misunderstood. It's sad that he had so little company in his thinking, especially given his craving for such company. *Wittgenstein Elegies* abides with him in that sadness. Or perhaps it's rather the wish to abide with him. If an elegy usually mourns something lost, it may also mourn what was not lost so much as longed for but out of reach, always absent. The poem had no chance of comforting the living Wittgenstein; that Wittgenstein was lost to the poem before it began.

Wittgenstein's thought also has something of the elegy about it. It reveals an ache at the heart of language, and in Zwicky's multiply elegiac poem, this ache may be what's hardest to bear. That famous final line of the *Tractatus,* "Whereof one cannot speak, thereof one must be silent," has a particularly bittersweet resonance because it comes after a book-length description of the very limited realm whereof one *can* speak. So much is left out:

> 6.421 *It is clear that ethics cannot be expressed.*
> *Ethics are transcendental.*
> *(Ethics and aesthetics are one.)*

So Wittgenstein tells us earlier in the *Tractatus.*

There is a sense in which the inexpressible is more precious for being so, for escaping language, for being wild. But as Zwicky observes in *Lyric Philosophy,* we are undeniably linguistic creatures.[12] Even as we may realize the beauty of the escape from language, we often *want* to speak. We sometimes go about it all wrong, "bang / like idiots against the bars of reason," trying force our way through to what won't be said.[13] But even speaking in the way Zwicky shows Trakl doing, gesturing toward the nameless, doesn't quite satisfy the longing to utter the world itself.

Language that knows this has elegy in its bones. In Zwicky's work, the inadequacy of language is an elegaic undercurrent even when it isn't named. But often it *is* named: a poem in *Forge* – Zwicky's most recent collection to date – begins, "I have spent too long / telling the world the world is the world / and poetry is made of language."[14] *Robinson's Crossing* is full of phrases like "the unwordedness / of beauty pressing up / through ordinariness"[15] and "joy / precise and nameless as that river / scattering itself among / the frost and rocks."[16] Or consider "Nostalgia," a poem that twists and turns, straining to name the quality of things remembered: is it – no, not that, nor that exactly … "full / somehow—but full of what? / The images swim up, sharp, / fragranced, but—like you— / behind a pane of glass."[17] Each failure becomes a gesture, pointing toward what the poem can't say.

Then there's *Songs for Relinquishing the Earth.* The very title, as well as mourning the global ecocide under way, is an invitation to imagine the Earth as always already receding, as ontologically beyond us insofar as it's beyond speaking. (In fact ecocide is partly the result of failing to perceive this.) The question is how, as linguistic creatures, to be graceful in the face of namelessness. And how to speak in a way that leaves room for the Earth's silence. That is what the *Songs* do, and it's where *Wittgenstein Elegies* leaves us – at the "emptied voice," in the "[s]alt light from over / the dark chafed sea." This sea is the Irish Sea off the coast of Galway, where the aging Wittgenstein wrote some of his last words and where the Wittgenstein of Zwicky's poem hopes for the courage to "love what must / each time we grasp it / vanish."

SUE SINCLAIR · Montreal, 2015

■ NOTES TO THE INTRODUCTION

1 Quoted by Ray Monk in *Ludwig Wittgenstein: the Duty of Genius* (New York: Free Press, 1990), 164.

2 Wittgenstein, *Philosophical Investigations,* trans. G. E. M. Anscombe (Oxford: Blackwell, 1978), §457.

3 Zwicky, *Songs for Relinquishing the Earth* (Victoria, BC: the author, 1996), 36.

4 Quoted by Ray Monk in *Ludwig Wittgenstein,* 291.

5 Monk, *Ludwig Wittgenstein,* 243.

6 Monk, *Ludwig Wittgenstein,* 291.

7 Monk, *Ludwig Wittgenstein,* 119.

8 Wittgenstein, *Tractatus Logico-Philosophicus,* trans. C. K. Ogden (London: Kegan Paul, Trench, Trubner, 1922), §4.112.

9 Zwicky, *Lyric Philosophy* (Toronto: University of Toronto Press, 1992), §18L.

10 Wittgenstein, *Philosophical Investigations,* viii.

11 Zwicky, *Lyric Philosophy,* §29L.

12 Zwicky, *Lyric Philosophy,* §116L.

13 Zwicky, *Wittgenstein Elegies,* 34.

14 Zwicky, "Lying Down in my Hotel Room, Thinking about the Day." *Forge* (Kentville, NS: Gaspereau Press, 2011), 23.

15 Zwicky, "Shabbiness." *Robinson's Crossing* (London, ON: Brick Books, 2004), 26.

16 Zwicky, "Glenn Gould: Bach's 'Italian' Concerto, BWV 971." *Robinson's Crossing,* 84.

17 Zwicky, "Nostalgia." *Robinson's Crossing,* 53.

WITTGENSTEIN ELEGIES

Among the unpublished writings Ludwig Wittgenstein left on his death was the typescript for a manuscript he called 'Philosophical Remarks'. A late draft of the foreword reads:

> *This book is written for such men as are in sympathy with its spirit. This spirit is different from the one which informs the vast stream of European and American civilization in which all of us stand. That spirit expresses itself in an onwards movement, in building ever larger and more complicated structures; the other in striving after clarity and perspicuity in no matter what structure. The first tries to grasp the world by way of its periphery — in its variety; the second at its centre — in its essence. And so the first adds one construction to another, moving on and up, as it were, from one stage to the next, while the other remains where it is and what it tries to grasp is always the same.*
>
> *I would like to say 'This book is written to the glory of God', but nowadays that would be chicanery, that is, it would not be rightly understood. It means the book is written in good will, and in so far as it is not so written, but out of vanity, etc., the author would wish to see it condemned. He cannot free it of these impurities further than he himself is free of them.*
>
> *November 1930*   *L.W.*

This expresses clearly and directly an aspect of Wittgenstein's work that is often neglected when that work is discussed by professional philosophers. If the following elegies manage to speak in some way to that absence, I will be glad.

PHILOSOPHERS' STONE

Immense turn in the deep black,
small points of light, faint gleam or slash
along some buried axis, white reticulated wink.
Size only guessed but staggering: swing
of infinite compounded rhythms through the
unthought reach. Each note pure, perfectly
distinct: the graveness of a star. Whom did this grow
within? Slow ramified unfolding, sky of a summer night
that hung the crystal arch above us, hummed silence.
But who is it that heard, who could have thought
that it might go like this about the rolling
piecemeal world? It is the possibility of life as art.
Analysis was never meant to hold
or judge: a purifier of the ore
it cannot comprehend. Don't rest
your weight on earth, for this
suspend yourself from heaven. Then
there will be light enough to leave untouched
the truth of each thing as it is.

We will be different.

□

The speech of plants is slow and still.
We are swum to over distances of light
like dreams. A patience. With all things
it is the same: each object shimmers with
its fundamental: anchor plumb in chaos.
But we are proud. Our deafness
wounds the world: braggart boots on meadow grass.

Find some way to prove, explain,
convince, some way to make
the common centre plain. Epiphanies that soar
transparent, frictionless. As glass.

☐

Grace is unmoved. It is the light that melts,
the spring where words and world
fill up with meaning. We will see things
stark and dead if we see only things
themselves and not the pattern that informs them.
What must be understood, not collectivity, not
substance, is the depth of an embrace.
Resist the great temptation. What rests within
without floats freely. By any words
the truth is unsupportable. To see
is to be unafraid to cast away the ladder
we have cherished.

☐

Webern's paradox: spare solitary
elements, yet each wound in the web that's torn apart,
then stitched, then fused, the gleaming cicatrix
become the very twisting of the thread.
Can one encounter fix the axis of a life?
A single glance, the brush of hands,
an indrawn breath: all specificities
preshadow loss, hold at their centre
absence, empty echo of the ardent voice.
When I have won through to the end, done
with the world, I shall have made it simple,

clear, the infinite variety of circumstance
set to one side so that in this,
my world, there will exist no tragedy.

    Words show us everything. How? Sense is
    vertical, position in the counterpoint.
    A necessary unity: aesthetics, ethics,
    truth. Whole presences in every word,
    the flicker of an eye.

☐

Love is despite the rock that is the world.
It spills, a tumbling careless wealth
across the granite face. The act of will
unspeakable: the world's own grief that grasps
the sweet ebullience, wrests it molecule by
molecule to build the crystal's heart,
painstaking day by day locks in the secret,
vast brilliant passion of the moveless glinting sea.

Stillness

THE DEATH OF GEORG TRAKL

I

Head down, imponderable coffee cold, the far reach
of lead-skyed November afternoons. His seriousness
a lump, a great huge lump:
he staggers underneath it like a saint.
What has he seen? Or do those eyes
see only through? He never speaks.
A sign, perhaps, a sign: the vacancy
of imbeciles, the simply mad or talented
is not so vibrant. Darkly luminous.

A stupid dream, all emptiness.
What we have seen is what the world acquires
from the strangeness of the way we see,
have seen, what we have heard:
mere echoes of ourselves, of others.

Ludwig
Wittgenstein

☐

Beautiful is the stillness of the night.
On a dark plain
We gather with shepherds and white stars.

When autumn has come
A sober clarity appears in the grove.
Calmed we wander beside red walls
And our round eyes follow the flight of birds.

Georg Trakl

☐

Sometimes he speaks: echoes.
He speaks echoes. So pure, almost
unrecognizable — and it's
what one must wish:
no clutter, stripped bare, colours
pure, original: unsayable itself
directly echoed. I have scraped and cut,
but unforgivable
the clumsiness. These limbless
sentences show nothing, little heaps
of rags and dust. Purity of heart
eludes me. Absence,
clear still space where truth might echo
chokes, these thick haphazard days.
My soul is made of sand, slides down itself,
collapses under every press of structure:
even, shapeless, yellow, same.
I cannot help these words as he can:
mute radiance, the empty shining valley.
I cannot keep them clean, they suffocate,
fall stillborn from my mouth.
Prod them for signs of life like poisoned mice.

☐

It is like this: We are asleep.
Our life is like a dream.
Only in better hours do we wake,
enough to realize we dream.
I cannot shake myself to consciousness.

At most I can endure, which is not courage
but the dumb strength of the body. What is

most simple has no way of being said, can only
show itself, a pure outstretch of arm. My words
are useless as my hands:
dream bodies move, but real ones do not stir.

II

Ludwig
Wittgenstein

Wealth clutters, opulence breeds death.
Enough to stay clean, sanity is nothing more. I'll
work. Give all the rest of it to art: the bright-souled
starve. But do not say
from whom to whom. Namelessness is
blessedness; what's hidden
does not interest us.

A philanthropic fluke, you think, a whim?
"Why use a jeweller's knife
to open orange crates?"
                                            Because you gawp
behind sealed windows, cannot know
what storm is raging, how a passerby
might have to struggle just to stand.
The truth is hidden, though it is
before you: simplicity once seen that is
most striking.
Pull the shutters. Leave me
stumble past your doorstep
dumb as stone.

☐

Tractatus Logico-
Philosophicus

Objects are simple. They are named
by simple signs. They are only named.
Signs are their representatives.
We can only speak about them,
cannot put them into words. In language
we can state only the how of things,

not what they are. What signs
fail to express, their application shows.
In logic, there is nothing accidental.
Somewhere the questions must be
simple, essence etched in every word.
There must be a realm in which the answers
a priori form a system:

                                  simplex sigillum veri.

What signs fail to express, their
application shows. If only
we are strong enough. The difficulty
is a difficulty of the will,
not the intelligence.

☐

What is seen in essence cannot be
immediately open to our view,
but something hidden, essence hidden
from us, unrecoverable by
artifice. Strict cleavages,
the lovely logic, winter mornings sunlit,
unrecoverable, buried in the background,
medium of understanding hidden.
Nothing can be explained or deduced.
It is all before us.

All that happens, all that
is the case, is accidental:

                        hardness
of the logical must.

Ludwig
Wittgenstein

Tractatus

Georg Trakl

Mighty are you, dark mouth
within me, shaped
from autumn clouds,
gold evening silence.
A greenly halflit mountain stream
in broken pines
that shadow place;
a village,
which dies piously in sepia.

Black horses leap there
in the misty meadow.
You soldiers!
From the hill, where the sun rolls dying
plunges the laughing blood —
under oaks
speechless! O thunderous melancholy
of the army; a gleaming helmet
rattled down from the purple brow.

So cool the autumn night comes,
shining with stars
above the broken bones of men
the silent solitary one.

☐

Stillness

Strung up like crows, he saw them
clear as night against the clear dawn,
black stretch, sharp as a caw against the sweet light

38

spread like a breath across a winter window.
Love of the weak ones, ninety,
on his hands, blood of the helpless.
By his own hand, stone agony.
He saw them. Frozen echoes, catch of breath.
Hung. Still. There. His.

☐

            Turn, world, against
the great clear space, against their innocence, his guilt,
at last unhidden eyes see through.
                      Turn, world, away
through emptiness to some blank place, smudged, filled
       with sand. Crumble
these shadows, indecipher them, make dust.

☐   ☐   ☐

But answers only clarity and light, mute
radiance of the shining valley.

Fill him now with pendant echoes,
pure impress of truth. His mouth turn, empty echo.
Offer. Burn the stone his eyes. Split
silent light, black aureoles.
Break, world, apart.

IV

Ludwig
Wittgenstein

Smooth sheets, cool golden afternoon
above the oak-furred ridge.
What failure does this signify, arrival
three days late? Cold forehead, temples thin
masked mirrors, blue bruise
of fingertips,

the silence.
Wild white silence.
A fence before the gate of heaven,
path of the extinguished angel.

So too at death the world does not alter
but comes to an end.

□

Tractatus

When the answer cannot be put into words,
neither can the question be put into words.
There are, indeed, things that
cannot be put into words. They make
themselves manifest.

Georg Trakl

We will never know
whether it is a strength or a weakness
to have survived where others could not.

Ludwig
Wittgenstein

Only what is simple is hidden:
the leaf in spring,
this gesture, the mind
of God.

40

IN THE ELDER DAYS OF ART

I

Rot even deeper than one thinks,
gone mushy to the core; no vision, only
words. Words, words, words, words.
Mere sketches, columns, lists;
a spelling book; a bunch of jigsaw
puzzle pieces cut by hand: all knobs
or none. But the structure was there,
surely, it was there — laid down, the matrix
grasped, scraped clean, fog
burnt away?
                    Mirage.
A fine and adult dream. No child
has handled forms so violent,
exquisitely seductive. Rough
innocence alone is in their fingers.
What they grasp, unpurified,
cracks on the adamantine face
of logic like a falling star.

☐

Gritty railroad din, the click, the rock
and shuffle. Silhouette against
the sooty window, back of his fingertips
brushing his chin, Italian disrespect, the
open palm: "Show me
the general form of proposition here, root
common structure!"
Answerless.
How is it possible to mean? I grope

through the rubble, mapless; brittle
scraps of thought whirl, eddy
in the sharp dry light like grains of sand.

The fleshless dead expose
the lie: burnt eyes, burnt lips
are motionless. Left lost, we bang
like idiots against the bars of reason
while beyond our reach they curl, blank rictus
stopped with earth. They leave inside us
rooms that have no keys.

II

Past in the Kundmangasse: hand work,
physical geometries. Did this not serve?
Slabs, pillars, blocks, and beams. There too
the unscarred minds of children whispered
in the sunlight. What was learnt? The trees
grew dappled in the afternoon high
overhead and hours blue at sunset when I was a child
the sky was song. Our muscles leapt,
strength was the easy supple bend of hope
in gardens cool at night beneath
an arch of stars.
                        How does one build
a living face? The woven laminae of flesh
and skin that quicken in a smile?
Lines have a history not copied
from a photograph; with age one turns,
folds over on oneself, dark valleys deepen.
In our sleep, small hands will
trace the crumbled courses wonderingly,
their fingers white and smooth.

□

Our language is an ancient city, maze of interlocking
streets and squares. To know it, we must
walk it, crawl through sewers, feel our way
by night along the walls. Most answers squat
before us, humble questions. Where they tower,
not the single-minded cleavage of broad-avenued

45

baroque, but subtler mysteries
reach heavenward, anonymous: the master-builders.

☐

Think of tools: a hammer, pliers,
glue-pot, glue, screwdrivers, saw,
nails, rule. So might we see
the purposes of words. Their
uniform appearance though
misleads us, tempts us
into superficial thought, sees
form in stasis rather than in life.

We order lives as houses, drift
along the cool black floors unshod,
a slender height of windows. None can speak
the truth who have not mastered their own souls:
our words are a refinement of our deeds. At root
the act, the open hand, like music pulls us to it,
grips us in a shadow of the world's embrace.
The green symmetry of plants is accidental,
means not end; and so our lives have system
not in structure but in function.
We are weavers, always weavers, of the cloth.
We draw the pattern after us, wind, wrap it,
in our simplest, most convolute of gestures.

☐

Work in philosophy is work upon
oneself. Slow chip and erasure,
fabric first grows rough, then thin,

the texture of a life. Rarely
under gentleness, unless another's, other
hands to bear the weight,
more seldom point the way.
                              So, solitary
work turns ritual, like ritual, rots
unless one clings to inner sense, digs
one's nails into the darkened core,
demands of every gesture that it be
as honest as an honest kiss.

III

Ludwig
Wittgenstein

Bright ligaments grow into bone just as
thought's fibrous tendons interpenetrate
the surer stuff of insight, wrap it round,
and finally make its shape their own.
But where the bone grows warped, and sinews
twine about the watery image of desire?
That we do mean, one overwhelming fact,
shall tear the axis of the universe
from stasis, wrench it live and open-mouthed,
about the fixed point of our need.

CONFESSIONS

The problem is: In what sense can we say
that logic is sublime? Thought is surrounded
by a halo. Logic, at its core, is prior
to experience, must be common both to world
and thought. The hardest thing there is.
                                We want to say:
"There can't be any vagueness." The idea
now absorbs us that the ideal
is concrete. One vast analysis, a single form
at each expression's root. We do not
yet see how it can occur — but
so superlative a fact!
                                We are seduced.
We think it must be in reality,
we think already that we see it there.
A thing that we had always known
but never spoken.
                                This was our mistake.

□

There is a general form of proposition:
This is how things stand. A simple structure
made of names and possibilities for truth.

What is the essence? What makes these sounds
a language or its parts? The general form
of propositions? No.
Nothing is common. All that we call
language, the phenomena in question, are

Philosophical
Investigations

Tractatus Logico-
Philosophicus

Investigations

51

related, one to others, differently.
Because of these relationships, we call them
language.
                    It is like a family.

                    □

*Propositions are truth-functions of
assertions of prime facts.*

*Assertions of prime facts
are simple thoughts.*

What dawned on me: logic is normative.
Living speech is not a calculus.
The most that can be said is: we construct
ideal languages.

Do away with explanation then.
Our task is to describe. We have only
to accept our words, our practices,
and note of false accounts that they are false.
Where our spade is turned, there we must rest.
Acceptance at the root. Ourselves.

A thought is a proposition with sense.

                    □

Certainty is of different kinds,
tones, colourings of thought.
"You're all at sea!" we say
when someone doubts a thing we recognize

as clearly genuine.
                    And yet we can prove nothing.
Can one learn this knowledge? Yes, some can.
But not by taking courses. It has rules
that form no system: life alone
learns to apply them right. Most difficult,
here, capturing indefiniteness, correctly and
unfalsified, in words. Imponderable evidence
includes all subtleties of gesture,
glance and tone. Gesture itself. foundation.

Perhaps if I could paint I might then show
the genuine and simulated glance in pictures.

Abstractions yield at best what will
appear to be the fragments of a system.

                    □

Although there is something arbitrary   Tractatus
in our notations, this much is not:
that when we have determined one thing
arbitrarily, some other thing
is necessarily the case.
                    Essence
is shown in general form.

          What we do in language always rests   Investigations
          on something that we take for granted, river
          in its bed.
                    Essence
          is grammatical.
                    As though

                                        53

by means of thoughts we catch
reality in nets.

A thought is a picture,
a logical picture of the facts.

Do I understand? Of course I understand.
I can imagine when you say it.
A picture does the service of the words.
And the service is the point.
But the picture does not point
to its own use. So we are taken in.
It takes us in. And what is to be done
or how this picture may be used
is still obscure.

□

If a sign is useless, it is meaningless.
That's Occam's point. And if
all things behave as though a sign had meaning,
then it does.

"How do sentences manage to represent?"
Don't you know? You surely see it
when you use them. Nothing is concealed!
"How do they do it?"
Don't you know? Nothing is hidden!
What has got to be accepted, what is given,
is a form of life. Our words are deeds.
"Have you not shut your eyes in the face
of doubt?"
They are shut.

54

Only in the nexus of a proposition
does a name have meaning.

Tractatus

□

It comes to this: only of a living human being

Investigations

and what resembles it, can it be said:
It sees, is blind, it hears, is deaf.
A smiling mouth smiles only in a human face.

Hence our attachments to our words.
We manifest these feelings by the way
we choose and value them.

The arrow points only in the application
that a living being makes of it.
                                    Yes.
To mean a thing is to go up to it.

What is the case — a fact —

Tractatus

is the existence of objects in combination.

□

Does each word carry with it

Investigations

a corona of lightly indicated uses,
delicate and shadowy hints of scenes?
If it is like this — if uses float
in half-shades as we say or hear some word —
this simply goes for us. We communicate
with others without knowing
if it is the same for them.

Pictures bewitch. A word's real use
compared with that suggested by the picture
will seem muddied. We have yearned for speech
designed for gods, a highway to the truth.
In front of us it shimmers. But of course
we cannot use it. It is permanently closed.

The possibility of each single case
discloses something of the essence of the world.

We walk into a room, our feet are bare.
Books, papers, letters, piled about,
discarded tie and random pencils,
picture crooked on the wall. At first
we think, "A mess! What disarray!
It should be straightened up!"
But then we look around and recognize
that no, no thing can be
disturbed. Even the dust is in its place.

☐

There is a general form of proposition:
This is how things stand.

One thinks that one has traced the nature
of a thing when really one has traced
the frame thorough which one sees it.
And when one draws a boundary,
there could be many reasons.

The world is all that is the case.

□

The silent path. The dappled shore.
Blue, blue the water.
Mist about the mountains.
How is it borne, a peace this tense,
world swelling like an ache?

Poised as the mist begins to lift.
Poised as the mist begins to lift.

A reach.

This is the very answer.

ROSRO, COUNTY GALWAY

Grooves in the rough-planed planks.
Trace the grain, back and forth, slow path,
back; and forth. Salt light from over
the dark chafed sea. So much is constant:
desk, cot, window. Wood, light, sea.
Trace, retrace, tide-worn wash of mind.
There is nothing left to strip away, grind
down, wear off: but still not pure enough, no
clarity. Words stumble, clutter, clog. I remain
a draughtsman; thought, dull pencil used
to trace the outlines that fragment and blur
at every stroke.

☐

The naked life is made of two:
the naked mind, the naked heart.
If only thought as well as art could force
the final gesture, that irrevocable moment of assent,
when fragments, haloed, coalesce
and the great space opens in the world
to make us simple.

   Signs by themselves are dead.
   What gives them life? Who teaches
   them to dance? In use they come alive.
   But where there is no courage,
   there can be no use, no speaking truth.
   Our mouths must move like fishes',

blank gapes
unfavoured by the breath of God.

□

It is evening when one hears most clearly.
Losses drop like pebbles in a shallow well.
A steady hand in the long-shadowed light
limns even the most delicate of ripples,
leaves each thing as it is.
Yet still the sickness, clumsy need
to wrestle with the pattern, make one blueprint
to explain all bricks.
                         But wholeness is a gift
of art, its essence transcendental.
The most that we can hope
is steadiness of soul, courage
to render with exactness what is set before us,
love what must
            each time we grasp it
                    vanish.

□

Grooves in the rough-planed planks,
                         over and over
voices, layered voices,
brilliant, chafing, lapping one another,
echo in the salt light. Great twisted rope,
the vision we will ride in flight
above the twilit world. How can we learn
to hear each one distinctly,
fragile threads in the enormous chorus?

□　□　□

And all that we have valued:
　　　　　　　　still high harmony
spare as the memory of November oaks
under an ancient sky.

□

Perhaps what is inexpressible is this:

　　The huge faint height beyond the shadowed heart
　　against which we must measure lives,
　　　　　the possibility of truth.

　　　　　Against which, only,
　　death might mean,
　　　　　　　the emptied voice

　　　　at last begin to speak.

Ludwig Wittgenstein had a varied career, ranging from engineer and primary school teacher to architect and Cambridge don. He served in both world wars, on the front in the first, and as a hospital orderly in the second. His major philosophical enquiries were centred on the nature of meaning, but in lectures, conversations, and journal entries, he also addressed questions of ethics, aesthetics, religion, mathematics, and psychology. During his lifetime he published only one book, the cryptic and allusive metaphysical system entitled *Logisch-philosophische Abhandlung*. (The Latin title of the English translation, *Tractatus Logico-Philosophicus*, was not Wittgenstein's idea, but G. E. Moore's.) Most of Wittgenstein's later views, such as those contained in the posthumously published *Philosophical Investigations*, appear to be a reaction against those developed in the *Tractatus*; and scholars continue to debate just what intellectual dynamic is involved. The relation between these works is complicated not only by the apparent discontinuity in the views, but also by difficulties in interpreting the views themselves. Wittgenstein did not present arguments in discursive essays; instead, he preferred to juxtapose dense, often highly metaphorical fragments, rarely more than a few sentences in length.

He was the youngest of eight brilliant siblings, children of Leopoldine Kalmus, an accomplished pianist, and the industrialist Karl Wittgenstein. His three elder brothers had committed suicide by the time Ludwig was in his mid-twenties, and he himself struggled with similar impulses all his life. As an adult, he was something of a hermit, frequently preferring the isolation of the Norwegian or Irish coast to either London or Vienna.

The intensity of his personality made a great impact on nearly everyone he met; and letters and anecdotes reveal that he was the victim of virtually unrelieved self-castigation. Yet when he died from cancer in 1951, aged sixty-two, his final words were, "Tell them I've had a wonderful life."

The poems draw on the following sources, often quoting them directly:

Paul Engelmann. *Letters from Ludwig Wittgenstein with a Memoir*, ed. B. F. McGuinness, trans. L. Furtmüller. Oxford: Blackwell, 1967.

Allan Janik and Stephen Toulmin. *Wittgenstein's Vienna*. New York: Simon & Schuster, 1973.

Norman Malcolm. *Ludwig Wittgenstein: A Memoir*. Oxford: Oxford University Press, 1984. [The 1984 edition contains Wittgenstein's letters to Malcolm.]

Georg Trakl. "Helian" and "Die Schwermut" in *Poems*. Athens, Ohio: Mundus Artium, 1973. [This edition of Trakl's poems contains *en face* translations by Lucia Getsi, from which my own translations have benefitted.]

Hermine Wittgenstein. Excerpts from family recollections in Bernhard Leitner, *The Architecture of Ludwig Wittgenstein*, New York: New York University Press, 1976. Essentially the same material appears as "My Brother Ludwig," trans. Michael Clark, in *Recollections of Wittgenstein*, ed. Rush Rhees, Oxford: Oxford University Press, 1984.

Ludwig Wittgenstein. *Culture and Value*, ed. G. H. von Wright in collaboration with Heikki Nyman, trans. Peter Winch. Chicago: University of Chicago Press, 1980.

———. "A Lecture on Ethics". *Philosophical Review* 74.1 (1965): 3–12. [Also reprinted in Ludwig Wittgenstein, *Philosophical Occasions 1912–1951*, ed. J.C. Klagge and A. Nordmann, Indianapolis: Hackett, 1993.]

———. *Philosophical Investigations*, trans. G. E. M. Anscombe, ed. G. E. M. Anscombe and Rush Rhees. Oxford: Basil Blackwell, 1958.

———. *Philosophical Remarks*, ed. Rush Rhees, trans. Raymond Hargreaves and Roger White. Oxford: Basil Blackwell, 1975.

———. *Remarks on Frazer's Golden Bough*, ed. Rush Rhees, trans. A.C. Miles, rev. Rush Rhees. Atlantic Highlands, NJ: Humanities Press, 1979.

———. *Tractatus Logico-Philosophicus*, trans. D. F. Pears and B. F. McGuinness. London: Routledge & Kegan Paul, 1972.

My warm thanks to Astrid Walter and Bruce Vogt for assistance translating Georg Trakl.

■ PHILOSOPHERS' STONE

Much of *Tractatus Logico-Philosophicus* was written while Wittgenstein was serving on the front in World War I, and later while he was a prisoner of war in Italy. In its form and content, it presents a striking contrast to the circumstances of its composition — the flyleaf describes it as a "vision of an inexpressible, crystalline world of logical relationships".

It brought its author instant acclaim in European academic circles when it was published in 1921, although its aim was gravely misinterpreted by logical positivists in both England and Vienna. Its logical sophistication had convinced them that it must be a defence of the positivist view that anything that cannot be characterized 'scientifically' should be discounted — whereas it was actually an attempt to demonstrate that all things of genuine value utterly supersede the world of 'facts'.

■ THE DEATH OF GEORG TRAKL

In 1914, the poet Georg Trakl received an anonymous donation from funds Wittgenstein had consigned to the editor Ludwig Ficker for distribution among promising young artists. Early in the war, Trakl, who was temperamentally unfit for military service of any sort, was placed in charge of a group of wounded soldiers for whom no medical supplies had been provided. His overstrained nerves collapsed following the suicide of the group's leader and his discovery, shortly after, of the hanging bodies of several men executed by the Austrian authorities. Trakl wrote to Wittgenstein from the psychiatric ward of a Kraków hospital, apparently having discovered the identity of his benefactor, and begged him to visit. Wittgenstein was unable to obtain leave immediately, however, and Trakl died, possibly by his own hand, three days before Wittgenstein's arrival.

▪ IN THE ELDER DAYS OF ART

The following jotting was made by Wittgenstein in 1938 and was later reproduced in *Culture and Value*.

> *Longfellow:*
>> In the elder days of art,
>> Builders wrought with greatest care
>> Each minute and unseen part,
>> For the gods are everywhere.

> (This could serve me as a motto.)

The middle period in Wittgenstein's development, which corresponds to the critical re-examination of the mechanics of the theory of meaning proposed in the *Tractatus*, also encompasses the period of his most intense architectural endeavours and his years as an elementary school teacher in Trattenbach, during which he compiled a spelling book. Kundmangasse was the street in which he studied for his teacher's certificate and, coincidentally, the street in which he later supervised the construction of the mansion he had designed for his sister Margarethe. The spur to Wittgenstein's rethinking of his views was provided by a gesture made by the Cambridge economist Piero Sraffa, during one of their many arguments about the views Wittgenstein had published in the *Tractatus*. The incident is rumoured to have taken place on a train.

The *Tractatus* is organized around seven central propositions; the remaining five hundred and nineteen propositions are all related to one of the first six, and the degree of their relations, as well as their relatedness to each of the other propositions falling under the same central proposition, is precisely indicated by a special number. The seven major propositions as they appear in the Pears and McGuinness translation are as follows:

1 The world is all that is the case.
2 What is the case — a fact — is the existence of states of affairs.
3 A logical picture of a fact is a thought.
4 A thought is a proposition with a sense.
5 A proposition is a truth-function of elementary propositions. (An elementary proposition is a truth-function of itself.)
6 The general form of a truth-function is $[\bar{p}, \bar{\xi}, N(\bar{\xi})]$.
7 What we cannot speak about we must pass over in silence.

The poem takes its title from Augustine's book of the same name, a work that Wittgenstein held in especially high regard.

■ ROSRO, COUNTY GALWAY

Rosro was a cottage near Renvyle, County Galway, which Wittgenstein rented in 1948, hoping to complete the manuscript of *Philosophical Investigations*. This hope did not prove well-founded owing, in part, to increasing ill-health. He had at the time three years to live.

Six years after publishing the first edition of *Wittgenstein Elegies,* I published a book of prose called *Lyric Philosophy.* I realized at the time that *Lyric Philosophy* was, in part, the poetics for *Wittgenstein Elegies.* What I hadn't noticed about *Elegies* — until I sat down recently and tried to sort out the dancing margins and half-blank pages of the original edition — was the extent to which it resembled *Lyric Philosophy* in being a collage of voices other than my own. In both books, a big chunk of the project involved displaying what others had said — in effect, pointing and saying listen to this! Here, in the second edition, I have pushed this element to the fore, giving names to the voices. The design, however, also includes a rule that separates the names from the text. The intent is to allow, simultaneously with the collagist reading, a reading more like that for which I was striving in the original edition: one that insists on the text as an integrated whole that ultimately overrides the multiplicity of voices. My hope is that the poem hangs together both as a kind of intellectual drama and as a piece of abstract music.

■ ■ ■

When I was a student in the '70s and '80s, there was a great vogue in Wittgenstein studies. This vogue has now passed, but back then, academic philosophers couldn't get enough of him. Wittgenstein, the person, had achieved mythic status in Oxbridge circles during his lifetime and this carried over into the decades after his death. My British-trained undergraduate professors treated his work with the reverence accorded Plato's and Hume's — that is, not much, but a great deal more than was accorded most others'. When I encountered him, Wittgenstein had already passed beyond the pale of 'thinking human being': he'd become a classic.

But he'd become a classic for the wrong reasons.

I read the *Tractatus* for the first time on a sunny, humid day in early September 1976. I'd just arrived in Toronto, a wet-behind-the-ears graduate student, and was doing some preparatory reading for classes that were scheduled to start in a week. As an undergraduate, I'd been exposed to several chunks of the so-called 'later Wittgenstein' — excerpts from *Zettel*, the *Blue and Brown Books* and *Philosophical Investigations* — as well as a raft of secondary pieces focussed on footnotes to others' footnotes on the main texts. I wasn't exactly chafing to dig in, but I knew I had to study more Wittgenstein if I wanted to be a serious philosopher; and so, amid the half-unpacked boxes, the windows open and St George Street booming beneath them, I settled in.

By the end of the first page, I was riveted. By the end of the book, I realized that the philosophical establishment had sold me a bill of goods. Wittgenstein wasn't an analytico. What was important about his work was that it drew limits to analysis; it put everything meaningful and valuable (correctly, in my view) outside the domain of direct articulation. Crucially, this didn't mean we couldn't *know* things about beauty or the good life. It just meant that if we tried to talk about them, we'd distort the truth. I dropped out of the class I'd signed up for and began reading in earnest.

What I read confirmed what I'd found in the *Tractatus*: Wittgenstein was neither a cynic nor a skeptic; he'd lived a life of tremendous moral intensity. And this was what I thought philosophy *ought* to do to a person: its study *ought* to help you see what mattered and what didn't; it should hone your appetite for a life saturated with the good. The misinterpretation of Wittgenstein's work, the then-current attempt to cram it into a positivist straitjacket, struck me as deeply unjust. I wrote *Wittgenstein Elegies* in an attempt to respond to this state of affairs. I wanted to draw attention to the unity of Wittgenstein's life and work. I hoped to show how profoundly he experienced the moral dimensions of language's relation to the world. Most importantly, I wanted to argue that his questions pose a fundamental challenge to anyone who wishes to take philosophy seriously. I called the result "Wittgenstein Elegies", but it might as usefully have been titled "On Language and the Good Life".

The poem hews closely to the public facts — Wittgenstein was a very private individual, and I respected this deeply. But it does juxtapose the facts in provocative ways, and it suggests links that are not explicit in Wittgenstein's own work. I now believe, some three decades later, that Wittgenstein himself would have advocated simply restating the facts, that he'd have kept putting them side by side, over and over again, until the light dawned. (For this reason, the poem in this sequence that I regard as most fully achieved is "Confessions".) And if the light didn't dawn? I'm not sure. Wittgenstein was also an impatient person. Perhaps he would have understood, if not approved of, my impulse to ventriloquize, to suggest links among the facts in an attempt to light them more insistently and dramatically.

The book is an attempt to imagine an experience of coming to the life of philosophy amid the collapse of post-Enlightenment European culture. The scope of cultural collapse has widened since Wittgenstein's day, and its velocity accelerates. In many quarters the idea of moral integrity has itself become a fiction — quaint, if not laughable. This, of course, creates a vacuum; and the vacuum provokes enraged but equally contentless reaction: the bleak absolutism of us versus them. In this regard, our predicament is even more dire than Wittgenstein's.

The lesson, however, remains the one he spent his life practising.

A NOTE ON THE TEXT

The first edition of *Wittgenstein Elegies* appeared in 1986, copublished by Brick Books in Ontario and Academic Printing and Publishing in Alberta. The speakers were unnamed in the first edition, and shifts from one voice to another were indicated purely by varying indents. For this edition, the author has revised the text substantially and chosen a new format to distinguish the multiple voices from one another.

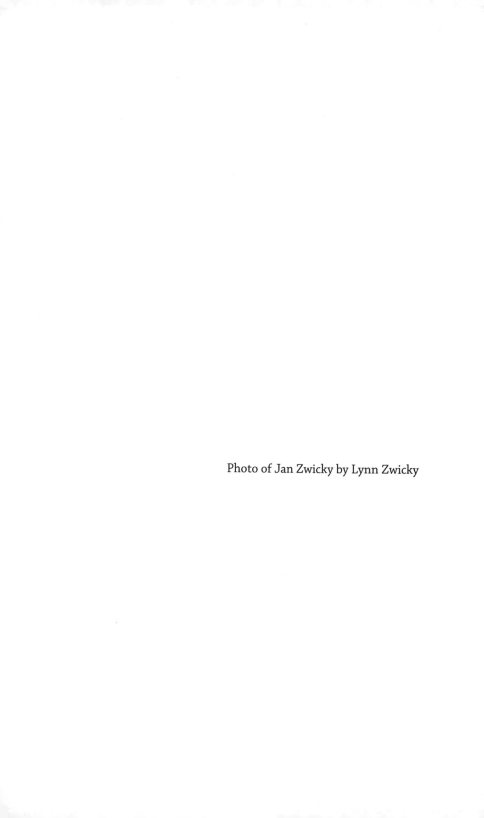

Photo of Jan Zwicky by Lynn Zwicky

JAN ZWICKY has published nine collections of poetry, including *Songs for Relinquishing the Earth,* which won the Governor General's Award, and, most recently, *Forge.* Her books of philosophy include *Lyric Philosophy, Wisdom & Metaphor,* and *Alkibiades' Love.* Zwicky grew up on the prairies, was educated at the Universities of Calgary and Toronto, and currently lives on the west coast of Canada. ¶ SUE SINCLAIR is the author of five books of poetry. Her latest collection, *Heaven's Thieves,* will appear with Brick Books in Spring 2016. She has a PhD in philosophy from the University of Toronto and works as an editor and teacher of poetry in Montreal.

Books in the Brick Books
Classics series are designed by
Robert Bringhurst. ¶ The text
face in this volume is Chaparral,
designed in California in 1997
by Carol Twombly. ¶ The type
on the cover is Palatino Sans,
designed 1973–2006 by Hermann
Zapf. The bricks were made in
the early 20th century from
Vancouver Island clay and aged
in the coastal rainforest.

BRICK BOOKS CLASSICS